A Project Based on Mental Health in the Greater Lansing Area.

1st Edition, Large Print

Lansing Riverfront Press

Special thanks to collaborative editing help from Charter House Members: Gary L., Michael R., Kenqua S., and John F.

Special thanks to Justice in Mental Health Organization Drop-In Center for hosting the Guest Speaker in Mental Health Engagements.

Thanks be to God for the inspiration.

GUEST SPEAKERS IN MENTAL HEALTH

BY

DANIEL K. ARNOLD

Guest Speakers in Mental Health:

Table of Contents

Daniel K. Arnold

Guest Speakers in Mental Health:

Chapter 1 - Defining Purpose

What goal do we have in mind when inviting guest speakers to mental health groups?

Inviting leaders to speak at a local mental health center effects more than just members; it provides a learning opportunity for the speakers as well.

Speakers should be carefully chosen not based on fame or politics, but to maximize mutual learning.

Dream big! What areas of interest do you think society and

mental health members are lacking in their knowledge set?

Are there items that should be addressed such as diseases, emergencies, health and social security income?

Perhaps, a guest speaker could put a new spin on topics swept under the rug because they are passionate and specialized in these topics. (Sometimes people other than the guest speaker(s) are afraid to address these issues.)

Remember, just as every mental health member is to be valued for bringing something unique to the table, so too can guest speakers be able to bring forth needed insight as outside perspectives.

Avoid downplaying the ideas of other members. Every view is to be valued and listened to fully.

Staff may make the final call on decisions, but as a guest speaker recruiter, voluntary or employed, everyone's opinion is to be given equal weight and consideration.

This is our job. This is our creed. Let's learn from one another.

Regards, Daniel K. Arnold and the Team

Chapter 1 - Small Group Engaging Questions:

1. What made you want to check out this workshop and become involved in recruiting guest speakers to your mental health center?

2. What goals does your team have in mind when inviting guest speakers to your mental health center?

3. What topics are important for your center to cover in a guest speaking engagement?

4. Can you think of any neglected topics that may be important to introduce that are

typically neglected in group settings?

Daniel K. Arnold

Guest Speakers in Mental Health:

Chapter 2 - Jumpstarting Initiatives

What do I do if I have a genius idea for a guest speaking engagement? Tell someone!
Yes. It is true. An idea is only a concept until it is shared.
Everyone has something different to bring to the table.
Mental Health involves an unlimited supply of unique topics that individuals or panels can lend their expertise to.

The importance does not lie on how important a person is, but on how crucial their message is to the advancement of the one-of-a-kind mental health drop-in center, clubhouse, Community Mental Health Authority, or educational gathering. What's important to you and your circle?

Let others voice their minds in think tanks so that every perspective can be addressed. Everyone's voice matters!

How do we bring great guest speaking engagements to our community? Will it disrupt the applecart? Sometimes yes. Sometimes cages will be rattled. Isn't making a difference what is important? Great ideas are formulated with hard work! Booyah!

Initiatives should not be proposed off the cuff to large audiences. They should be carefully planned and involve assistance whenever necessary. I have an extra brain helping me with editing right now and bright ideas. Thank you Michael R. (The more brainstorming of ideas, the more productivity will occur.)

When the initial core group is formed to share ideas, no matter how large or small the group, it is time to set aside time to meet. Be considerate of as many people's availability as possible, but do not procrastinate dates to the point of losing audience attention.

The group's first goal should be to gain the approval of the center that the speaking engagement will be taking place at. Be mindful that they probably already have a structured schedule in place. Think about making sure that some of the leadership from the center are able to attend (usually normal business hours) the meeting that will be scheduled for the speaking engagement.

It is my opinion that leaders who receive this proposal should not be crowded, but have the idea for speaking engagements presented to them by just one or two people at a time.

Be excited. Have fun with this. You have the potential to make great waves as a member and friend!

Chapter 2 - Small Group
Engaging Questions:

1. Do you have any ideas to help accommodate those who have trouble speaking up about their interests?

2. How can we encourage other members to speak up and get involved in the guest speaker recruitment process?

3. How will you propose new ideas for guest speaking at your local mental health center? Will you develop a focus group? What will be discussed in this group?

Daniel K. Arnold

Guest Speakers in Mental Health:

Chapter 3 – First Impression Communication

Hello. My name is Daniel. It is great to meet you. Let me share what is important/crucial to me and my community! I know you may be busy, but I am convinced that you have something magnificent to bring to the table and so do I.

May I have five minutes of your time?

There is no cookie-cutter way to initiate first impression communication with potential guest speakers. However, respect and consideration are always needed.

Do not be shy. Bring yourself to the game. Prepare and tell the person in summary format just why you need the help of his/her organization, company, or non-profit. Be ready to receive assistance from a leader's assistants. Do not demand participation from just the CEO, but keep an open mind for him or her to delegate participation to others. This will keep options open and maximize the opportunity for participation.

For instance, I met the Lansing Chief of Police at a speaking engagement at Sycamore Creek

Church to open bridges of understanding to reduce racial discrimination. I waited until after the meeting to speak to him about speaking at Justice in Mental Health Organization. I found it necessary to arrange a meeting between him and the JIMHO Community to open lines of communication and understanding in regards to mental health with the police.

As much as I personally wanted his personal one-on-one participation at JIMHO, he was too occupied to show up on short notice. Yet, he did not give up on us. Instead, Chief Michael Yankowski did a splendid job of quickly delegating the meeting to multiple levels of authority below him with the Lansing Police Department. When the event took place, there was a captain, a sergeant, a community policing negotiator, and a community policing officer present for an outstanding meeting!

What type of media do you use in communicating with a potential guest speaker first is up to you. I always believed I was better at written communication than oral, but with practice I have improved on tele-communication. As professionals may say, "The best format is usually face-to-face," but if for some reason you seem unable to do that, do not let it stop you!

Nothing can stop the determined member. Contact people in a professional manner with phone calls, e-mails, written letters, face-to-face, conference speaking, Facebook—whatever method penetrates the lines.

It is true that I was unable to receive a reply from the Lansing Mayor's Office. This is somewhat understandable being that I am a pretty much unemployed person appealing to the Mayor of the Capital City of Michigan. However, I persisted! I did not give up. I pressed my plea. I called and sent four e-mails. When this method of media contact did not work, I looked up Virg Bernero, the Mayor of Lansing, on Facebook Messenger.

Transcript:

Virg Bernero (Public Figure)

November 12, 2016 AT 12:01pm

"Do you feel your office is too important to advocate for mental health?"

The question I posed was a bit loaded, but I remained polite. I went straight to the point and was somewhat surprised at his long thoughtful response. Victory!

I would find this initial win to be just the start of my journey in establishing the Mayor of Lansing as a guest speaker in mental health.

Thanks for listening!

Chapter 3 - Small Group
Engaging Questions:

1. How will you open dialogue
with guest speakers in authority?

2. Practice with your small group
in a circle. Pretend you are
communicating with someone
fascinating to propose a guest
speaking engagement to for the
first time.

3. What will you open with?
How will you introduce your
agenda? How will you close the
conversation? Delegate to one
person in your group to share this
experience with our group…

Daniel K. Arnold

Guest Speakers in Mental Health:

Chapter 4 – Follow-Up

The old adage goes as follows,
"If at first you don't succeed, try,
try again." This saying is
especially applicable when
proposing guest speakers at
mental health centers. Yay!
The verbal agreement for a
meeting is just the beginning.
Relationships, even professional
ones, must be delicately built and
maintained.

Many times, guest speakers
become quite pre-occupied and
are hard to reach. Multiple types
of media outreach have to be

used to breakthrough and maintain contact. Be careful to remain polite, but remember persistence and tenacity pay off!

I enjoy continuing communication with friendliness. I like to give updates on my progress and ask the speaker how he/she is doing.   Know that all communicators are only human and desire to be reached on a personal level. Strive to relate in a personable way to everyone you come in contact with in the setup process.

If a leader, like the police chief seems occupied, contact those who he/she has delegated authority to in the speaking engagement.

Do not quit! The worst result that could happen is a cancellation. Do not burn bridges as many times life happens. There should be no hard feelings when a busy professional has to reschedule. Be patient and be ready to schedule in other speakers in the original speakers' places.

When I set up the follow-up with Mayor Virg Bernero, there was an initial delay and rescheduling. It seemed frustrating at first, but persistence was well worth it when he showed up and engaged the audience of Justice in Mental Health Organization.

Mayor Virg Bernero actually appreciated that I never gave up and pressed my plea. He congratulated me on my tactics to make sure he was present at the meeting. I gave him periodic updates about how people in the mental health community in Lansing were doing. I displayed videos communicating to the Mayor about homelessness in his hometown. He was moved by these videos and showed a lot of compassion.

Similarly, when I communicated with the Capital Area Transportation Authority

(CATA) Bus Station about a complaint, a lot of persistence was necessary. I tried all avenues to communicate my complaint and when they did not work as I planned, I went to the administration building. An individual in the complaint department ended up offering to meet with JIMHO and I was delighted/highly encouraged!

I find that when you have to persist and take issues up the ladder, you have the opportunity to become acquainted with more people in authority. This can be exciting and rewarding. Never give up!

Chapter 4 - Small Group
Engaging Questions:

1. What is your favorite form of media outreach?

2. What seems to work the best and why?

3. Give an example of some diverse way you have contacted another agency that was stretching for you. Why was it stretching? Why was it rewarding?

Daniel K. Arnold

Guest Speakers in Mental Health:

Chapter 5 – The Main Event

After all this hard work, after all this planning, what's next? Of course planning the main event is next. Who will speak is just the beginning... There are other considerations as well.

A guest speaker recruiter must find someone to facilitate the meeting. Perhaps, he/she does not specialize in that skill. At JIMHO, I received a lot of help in group facilitation from a certified peer support specialist who specialized in groups at her job.

Yes, I initially opened the meetings, but she did some follow-up during lull times.

In the event that no facilitator can be provided, preparation is always the best policy. As the slogan goes in life, "The buck stops here." Meaning, those who lead up a meeting are responsible for how it is carried out.

This can be a real stretching yet rewarding opportunity. Remember that you are among friends. Do not overstress.

Presentations for different guest speakers come in different formats. A representative from the Michigan Disability Rights Coalition did a presentation on appealing to politicians through PowerPoint. There should always be time set aside for a question and answer session.

This session can be a very fruitful learning opportunity for both the speaker and the participants at a mental health center. Do not underestimate the power of curiosity and a great speaking team.

The Lansing Police Department engaged the audience from start to finish with an outstanding explanation and Question & Answer session. The time spent was powerful. Make sure to be well-planned and inform staff and members ahead of time of the great opportunity ahead in a guest speaking engagement. Thank you and have a great day!

Chapter 5 - Small Group Engaging Questions:

1. Introduce a sample group facilitation guest speaker question to our group.

2. How would you word the question as to bring about understanding to the mental health center and stimulate dialogue from the guest speaker?

3. Have you ever had a lull period during an important meeting that intimidated you? How do you recover from this scenario? Did you delegate authority? Explain your experience.

Daniel K. Arnold

Guest Speakers in Mental Health:

Chapter 6 – Lull Period

What do you do during the period when planning stops? What do you do when you do not know what the next step is for planning special event guest speaking at your mental health center?

This is what's known as the Lull Period. Hmm… Do not quit! Continue to ask others for feedback. Do your research homework. What is important to your community and mental health center? Find out! Get assistance.

"When the Lull Period comes to you, you have to go outside the box to accomplish your purpose and goals which you feel inspired by. My Lull Moments come when I'm alone—better yet, isolated, but I ask for help from God to give me revelation on how to attack and achieve my dreams," says Kenqua S..

I agree it is important to dig deep during a Lull Period—to find a place of solace and take care of matters that might be neglected.

Group collaborative thought is helpful too. It might be a good time to revisit a think tank group and brainstorm ideas.

It is also helpful to try new activities outside of your comfort zone. I found that I discovered new ideas by attending a mental health clubhouse. I learned much at my local mental health drop-in center, but there were new angles to explore when I became acquainted with a new mental health outreach group.

"Make new friends, but keep the old. One is silver and the other gold." This song applies to expanding perspective on any subject matter.

Today I brought a new person to the circle of group collaboration to this book and he reminded me to take time to myself and explore my spirituality. Thank you Kenqua S.!

Chapter 6 - Small Group Engaging Questions:

1. What is your worst fear when facing a planning Lull Period?

2. How do you overcome that fear?

3. What role does group collaboration play in group events at your mental health center?

4. Think with your small group something that might be lacking in your group events/guest speaker meeting agenda.

Daniel K. Arnold

Guest Speakers in Mental Health:

Chapter 7 – Thank You's

To Whom It May Concern:

I appreciate you taking the time to participate in this guest speaking engagement. You truly made a difference.

Kind Regards,

Daniel K. Arnold

The more personalized a "Thank You" greeting the better. The handwritten Thank You card is a great personal touch. If people/professionals are hard to reach, e-mail will work, but a personal touch is always the best method.

Keep in mind that the door may be open for a future guest speaking engagement—in a year, in six months, whatever fits your schedule and theirs.

Be sure to include in a Thank You that you and your mental health center would look forwards to future engagements if this is the case.

Be creative. Put quality into preparing your Thank You. People/professionals appreciate us putting care into our work.

Enjoy yourselves. This is a time to celebrate a great speaking engagement!

Chapter 7 - Small Group Engaging Questions:

1. What does your group believe is important to put into a guest speaking engagement Thank You?

2. How would you respond to guest speaker who spoke who did not respond to follow-up?

3. How would you respond to a guest speaker that didn't present as you wanted?

4. Would you still say, "Thank You?" Why or why not?

Daniel K. Arnold

Guest Speakers in Mental Health:

Chapter 8 – Conclusion

So you have considered arranging a guest speaking engagement for your mental health center? Hopefully, this guide has given you some ideas for who to talk to and where to begin.

Remember, this activity is supposed to be fun. It is meant to raise awareness and spur on mutual learning, but it is also meant to be enjoyable. Make sure you do not pressure anyone in the process, but take things as they come.

Your efforts matter; your voice matters; mental health matters! Thank you for listening.

Kind Regards,

Daniel K. Arnold

Take Away Small Group
Engaging Questions:

1. What have you learned today about guest speaking engagements that you can bring back to your mental health center?

2. What questions do you still have in your mind?

3. What will be the first guest speaking engagement that you plan to host?

4. Do you have any additional comments?